"Not you again...!"

Helping children improve playtime and lunchtime behaviour.

by

Fiona Wallace & Diane Caesar

Lucky Duck Publishing
34 Wellington Park
Bristol BS8 2UW

Phone or Fax 0117 9732881 or 01454 776620
e-mail publishing@luckyduck.co.uk
website www.luckyduck.co.uk

ISBN 1 873942 95 8
Fifth Printing February 1999

Notes for guidance

Introduction

These worksheets and activities have been devised to help teachers and dinner supervisors work with primary school children who are in trouble at dinner and play time. Some of the principles which guided the development of the materials are listed below:

- Adults can help children improve their behaviour without resorting to punishment or strategies based on deprivation of pleasurable activities or learning experiences.

- Staff must be able to deal effectively with a child in trouble without automatically attributing blame to the child or their actions.

- Children should take responsibility for their own actions ..... both those that get them into trouble and those that they can take to change their behaviour 'for the better'. The worksheets provide a set of exercises which encourage children to think about themselves and their actions in a constructively critical manner and provide opportunities to learn new skills which are less likely to get them into trouble.

- No child should be 'written off' as beyond help and neither is any child perfect. There is always the chance to develop or strengthen skills and relationships and improve on behaviour.

- Resources for busy teachers must be easy to use. Not you again ! is ready to use. The purpose of each worksheet is clearly stated and sheets can be freely copied within the purchasing establishment. The blank borders enable new sheets to be quickly designed which will complement the published pack.

The book is divided into three parts. Section one is a collection of general worksheets that have been designed to address specific problem behaviours that occur in all playgrounds in all schools, spoiling others games, dropping litter and so on. Section two contains sheets that are most suitable for the child who is often in trouble and the final section comprises a key copy of each of the borders so that schools can build up a bank of additional worksheets designed for specific problems or particular individuals.

The worksheets can be used in any way that suits your particular school and staff may choose the sheets most appropriate to each individual child's ability and needs. It is not intended that the materials will cover every problem behaviour that occurs outside the classroom. Other sanctions will still be appropriate and some behaviours will be too serious to be dealt with using these materials.

Before you start

The procedures agreed for the use of the materials should be discussed and included in the school behaviour policy. You should consider the following questions:

- Who should give out the worksheets?
- Where they are to be done?
- Who is to supervise their completion?
- What happens to the finished sheet?
- What records are to be kept?
- Who decides to begin to use materials from the second section of worksheets?
- Are the procedures for using worksheets from this section the same?
- When and how will parents be involved?

It is important that staff agree with the principles which guided the development of the book (outlined above) and other principles fundamental to effective pupil management, such as the need to handle behaviour consistently and to reinforce positive behaviour. You may find this short selection of activities helpful in exploring views and gaining agreement amongst staff, both teaching and non-teaching. The reference list gives sources of other activities.

1. Looking at problem behaviour

As a whole group brainstorm a list of all the problem behaviours that occur in your playground . Divide into smaller groups and work together to distribute each problem behaviour into one of the four quadrants of this diagram:

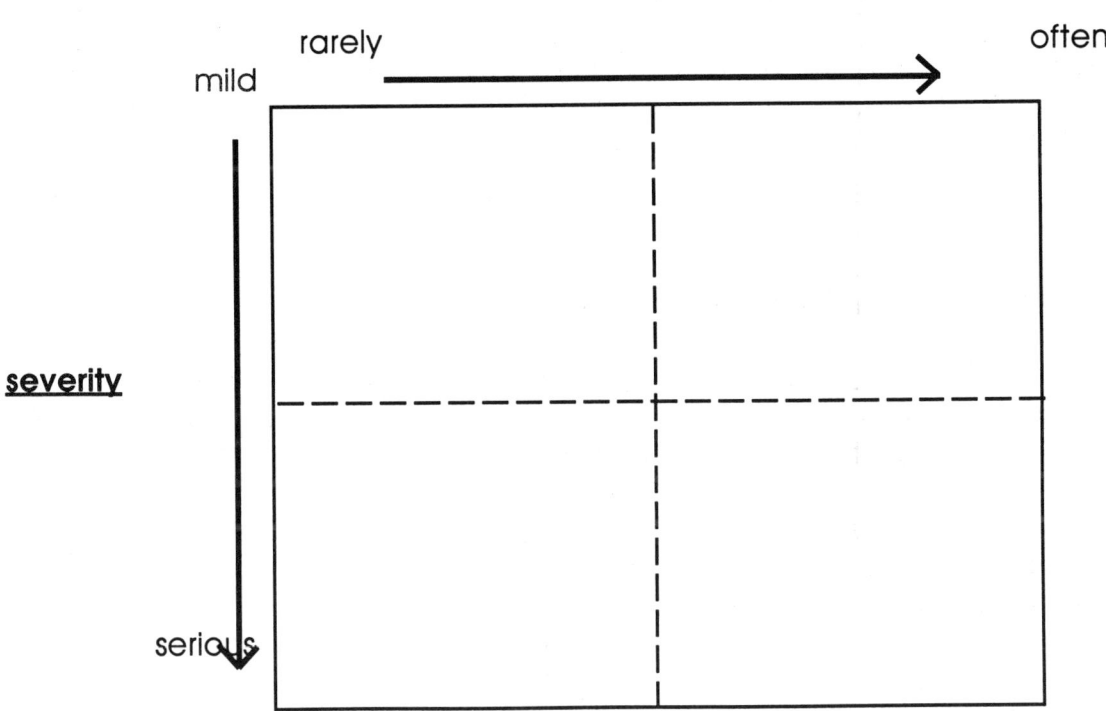

The results of the deliberations of each group can then be discussed in order to try to gain agreement across all staff as to the priority behaviours to target first.

2. Agreeing strategies

Brainstorm a list of all the strategies which could be used to deal with difficult behaviour. Agree a coding system and mark each strategy according to:
- how frequently it should be used (sometimes, often, never)
- for which age groups
- by which staff (classteacher, head, dinner supervisor, etc.)

Make any further comments at the side of each strategy. Write up the results of this exercise and distribute copies to all relevant staff with a reminder to stick to the agreements made.

3. Seeking pupils' views

Share your list of the most commonly used strategies for handling difficult playground behaviour with groups of pupils. Ask if the strategies are considered effective and fair and if they have any other suggestions. Alternatively use your list of problem behaviours and ask the pupils to match appropriate sanctions to behaviours. This is best done in groups rather than individually.

4. Observing playground behaviour

Much information and many ideas can be generated just by systematically watching what goes on in the playground. Pupils and staff can observe themselves and each other or you may want to ask an outsider, perhaps your school educational psychologist. You might look at the following:

- The use of the playground, for example which games are played by whom and where?
- What do staff do? Do they interact with the children, where do they stand, how many positive comments are made to pupils?
- Are there any patterns to problems? Are there good days and bad days? Where and when, exactly, do difficulties occur?

Make the observations over a reasonable period of time and then gather the information and in discussion with pupils and staff see if changes to current practice are indicated.

SECTION ONE - General worksheets

Over thirty photocopiable sheets are included which encourage the child to reflect on the particular behaviour that has got him or her into trouble and, more importantly, to consider more appropriate behaviour.

The worksheets in this and the following section should be enjoyable for the child. Although many children will have been 'sent in' to complete a sheet, the worksheet itself should not, if possible, be seen as a punishment. Children should be given every opportunity and appropriate support to complete worksheets successfully.

Children should not be routinely denied all their break time - they need an opportunity to let off steam outside. Each worksheet should therefore occupy a child for no more than 10 to 15 minutes. For those who are quicker the detailed border can be coloured in to enhance the finished sheet. Only pencils and crayons are needed and most children should be able to work independently, perhaps after a little help to read the worksheet through and get started.

When a child is sent in from the playground to complete a sheet they should be quite clear what they have done wrong. It is often helpful to ask the child why they are in trouble so that misunderstandings can be cleared up immediately. A worksheet appropriate to the misdemeanour can then be selected and discussed with the child. As there are likely to be some persistent 'offenders' a record should be kept of who has done which sheet. It will be helpful to date this list so that sheets may be repeated after a interval if necessary.

Once completed, the child should be praised for their work and the sheet signed and dated at the bottom. It is important that staff value the task and the efforts of the child, to help the child remember the message contained in the worksheet. A comment recording any discussion about the problem behaviour might be noted on the back of the sheet. The completed worksheets should be kept as a record of work toward helping a child alter their behaviour. They might usefully be shared with parents.

SECTION TWO - The child who is often in trouble

In every school there will be a few children who are frequently in trouble; there is always someone who always seems to be in the wrong place at the wrong time!

The child who is often in trouble may need help to see that there are alternative ways of thinking and acting which are less likely to get them into trouble. They should learn to think about themselves and be urged to take responsibility for their actions. Children should be encouraged to believe that they can find solutions to their problems. They should be taught that there is always the chance to develop or strengthen relationships with either their peers or the adults they come into contact with.

There are three groups of worksheets in this section:

- those designed to elicit information about the children, for example their views about themselves, their friendships, likes and dislikes. This information may shed light on some of the factors precipitating difficult behaviour and should assist in planning for change in the child's behaviour.

- those designed to help the child focus on what he or she actually does at breaktimes and, in particular, what it is that gets him or her into trouble.

- those designed to teach new skills and more positive attitudes.

For the worksheets in these sections it is suggested that a member of staff works with the child, particularly if he or she is in a younger age group, or carefully reviews the completed sheet with them, to draw out any information that might be used to help modify behaviour. Where problems are common to a group of children the worksheets could be done individually and then discussed in small groups of two or three.

As with the general worksheets the child's completed sheets should be valued by staff, signed, dated and kept safely. It is important with some of the sheets to respect information the child has given which may be misinterpreted if it gets out to a wider audience. For example who the child dislikes or who gets him or her into trouble.

Further help and ideas

There are several publications available which address difficult behaviour in the playground, either directly or indirectly. You may like to browse through the selection below. To guide your choice brief notes are included on each.

Ross, C. and Ryan, A. 1990
"Can I stay in today, Miss?" Improving the school playground. Trentham Books.

> This book describes strategies and procedures that may significantly change behaviour on the playground, reducing aggression and abuse among children and giving girls fair access to playground space. The strategies range from classroom discussions to redesigning the entire playground.

Lunchtime Supervision. Oxfordshire Program for Training, Instruction and Supervision (OPTIS), 1991. Available from: The Sales Director, OPTIS House, Cricket Road, Oxford, OX4 3DW.

> The 36 pages in this booklet are designed for dinner supervisors to work through. There are checklists to fill in, examples of what might happen to think about, information to find out and questions to answer.

Luton, K., Booth, G., Leadbetter, J., Tee, G. and Wallace, F. 1991
Positive Strategies for Behaviour Management. NFER Nelson.

> Scripted sessions, handouts and overhead transparencies are included in this pack which can be used in a variety of ways by primary school staff. The materials provide a clear positive framework within which staff can work together to develop their own effective behaviour management strategies.

Galvin, P., Mercer, S. and Costa, P. 1990
Building a Better Behaved School. Longman.

> The nine units in this pack are designed to be used by primary schools to help them develop policy, procedures and practice which will promote social relationships in school.

Practice to Share: The management of children's behavioural needs.
National Primary Centre (Westminster College, Oxford, OX2 9AT) in conjunction with Birmingham City Council.

> Four booklets are included in this pack, one of which covers the management of the midday break within a whole school context. The pack, which is undated, was published as a result of a project in Birmingham in 1988.

Blatchford, P. 1989
Playtime in the Primary School: Problems and improvements.
Nelson, 1989.

> Easily read, this book reports on the relevant research and guides the reader in ways of improving the primary school playground and playground behaviour.

Blatchford, P. and Sharp, S. [eds.] 1994.
Breaktime and the School. Routledge.

> A valuable addition to Blatchford's earlier work, this book contains contributions from several authors and will encourage teachers to consider the arrangements and dynamics of playtime and playspace.

Contents

*A companion publication "What else can I do with you?" to support classroom management is now available from Lucky Duck Publishing.

"Thank you"

is a polite thing to say in any language.

Colour all the words
carefully

Gracias

Merci

Tak

Danke

Grazie

"Please"

is a polite thing to say in any language.

Colour all the words
carefully

Bitte
German

Ludzu
Latvian

Si'l vous plait
French

Por favore
Italian

Signed

Date

Make a poster to remind all the children about the playground rule:

We play safely in the playground without kicking.

Imagine that your class has won the school trophy for the best behaviour. Write down what you did to win.
Draw the trophy

Our Class..

Class Behaviour
Trophy

Signed

Date

Make a word search. Put in all these things which you can do in the playground without being told off!

run   skip   smile   laugh

chatter   jump   play   walk

sing   hop   dance   talk

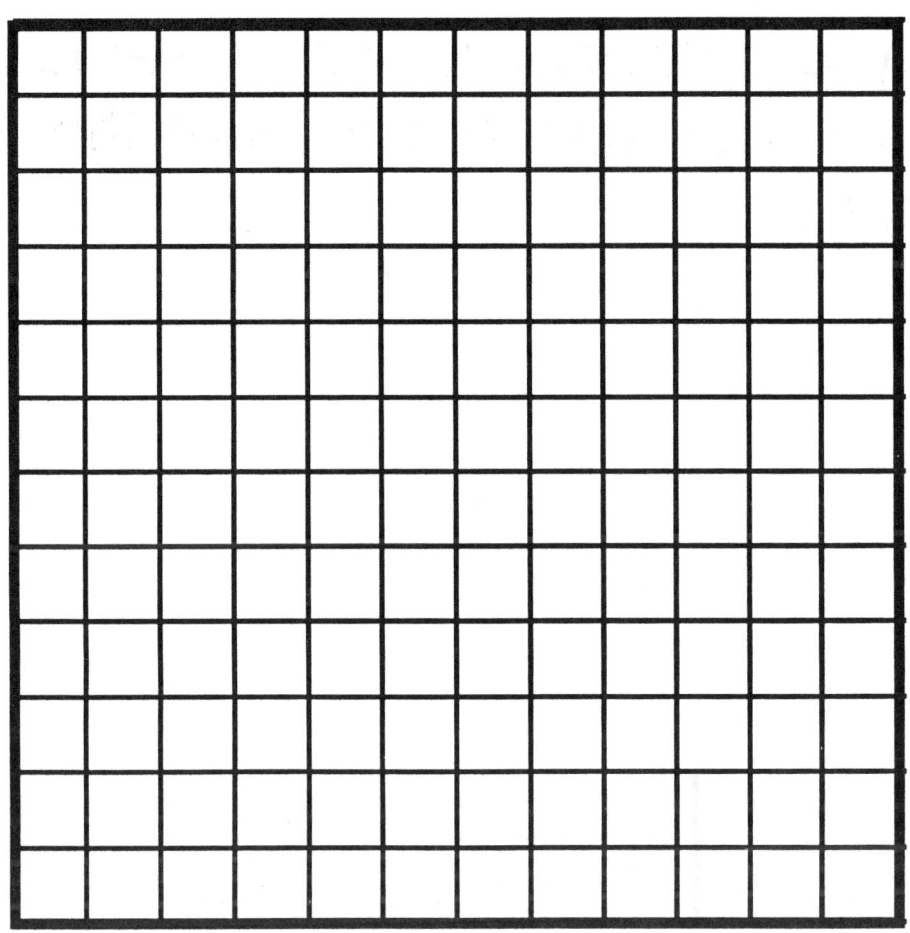

Daily Newspaper

Dinner Lady is a heroine at school.

Yesterday at a local school a dinner lady, pictured above, was cheered by pupils. Our reporter continues the story.....

Signed   **Date**

Word Search

f	r	i	e	n	d	l	y	a	b	e	s
s	u	o	e	t	r	u	o	c	l	v	t
s	y	z	a	r	q	f	u	t	c	p	h
e	n	x	f	w	d	r	n	c	v	g	o
n	e	e	u	d	q	e	o	p	e	a	u
s	o	w	n	x	g	c	t	n	l	b	g
i	e	t	i	l	o	p	e	m	b	k	h
b	l	g	k	f	y	r	o	z	s	k	t
l	m	o	i	j	o	g	h	t	i	j	f
e	j	o	h	u	i	l	n	n	d	u	u
k	n	d	s	m	g	f	d	h	i	e	l
e	c	i	n	g	c	a	r	e	f	u	l

friendly   thoughtful
kind   generous
polite   fun
gentle   careful
nice   good
sensible   courteous

Crack the code to discover this message and write it in the box.

A B C D E F G H I J K L M

N O P Q R S T U V W X Y Z

Now write another helpful message in code

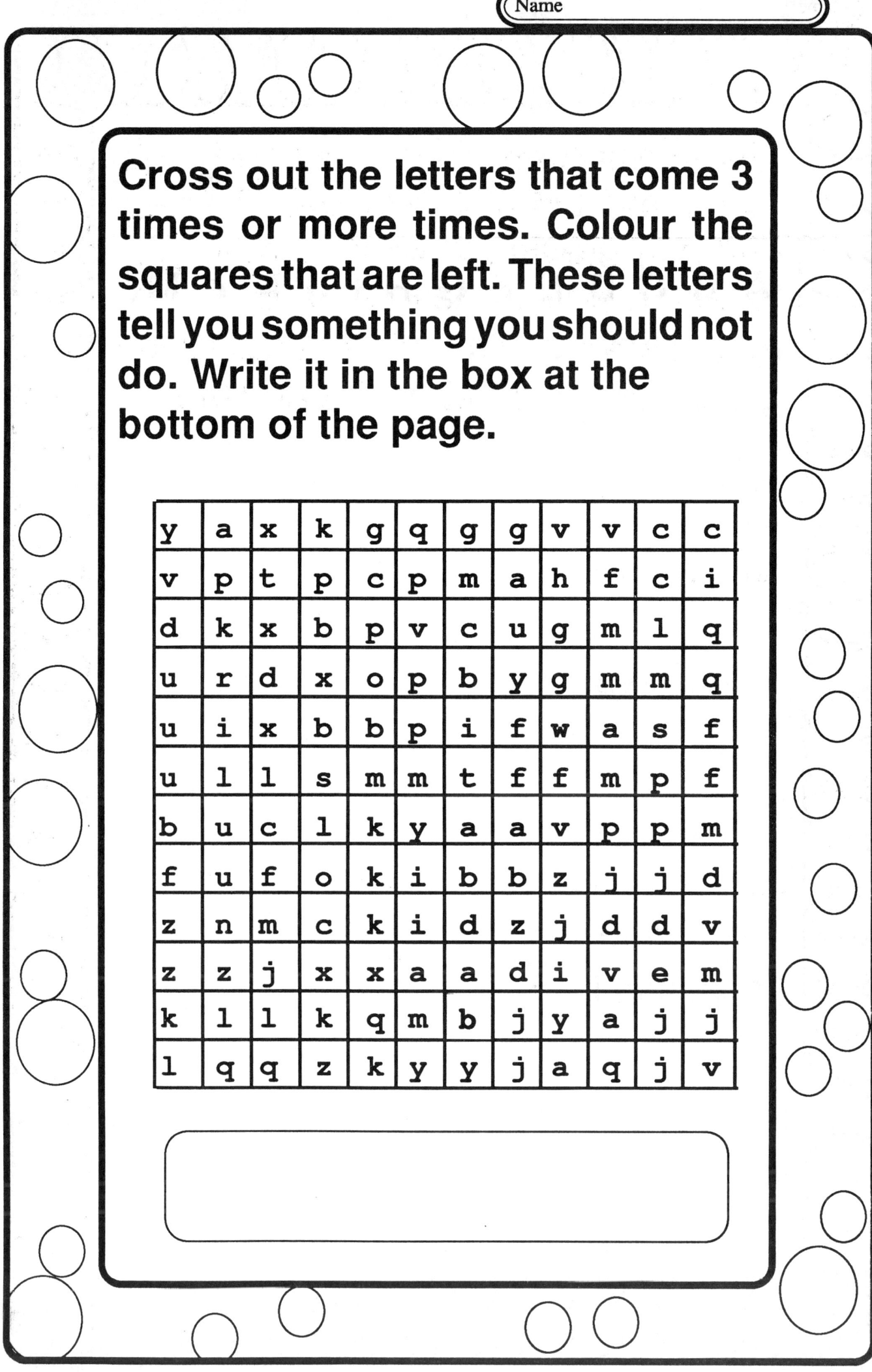

Cross out the letters that come 3 times or more times. Colour the squares that are left. These letters tell you something you should not do. Write it in the box at the bottom of the page.

y	a	x	k	g	q	g	g	v	v	c	c
v	p	t	p	c	p	m	a	h	f	c	i
d	k	x	b	p	v	c	u	g	m	l	q
u	r	d	x	o	p	b	y	g	m	m	q
u	i	x	b	b	p	i	f	w	a	s	f
u	l	l	s	m	m	t	f	f	m	p	f
b	u	c	l	k	y	a	a	v	p	p	m
f	u	f	o	k	i	b	b	z	j	j	d
z	n	m	c	k	i	d	z	j	d	d	v
z	z	j	x	x	a	a	d	i	v	e	m
k	l	l	k	q	m	b	j	y	a	j	j
l	q	q	z	k	y	y	j	a	q	j	v

The playground should be a place to have fun and play games, or even to take a walk or have a rest. Draw a plan of a great playground. Write what each part is for.

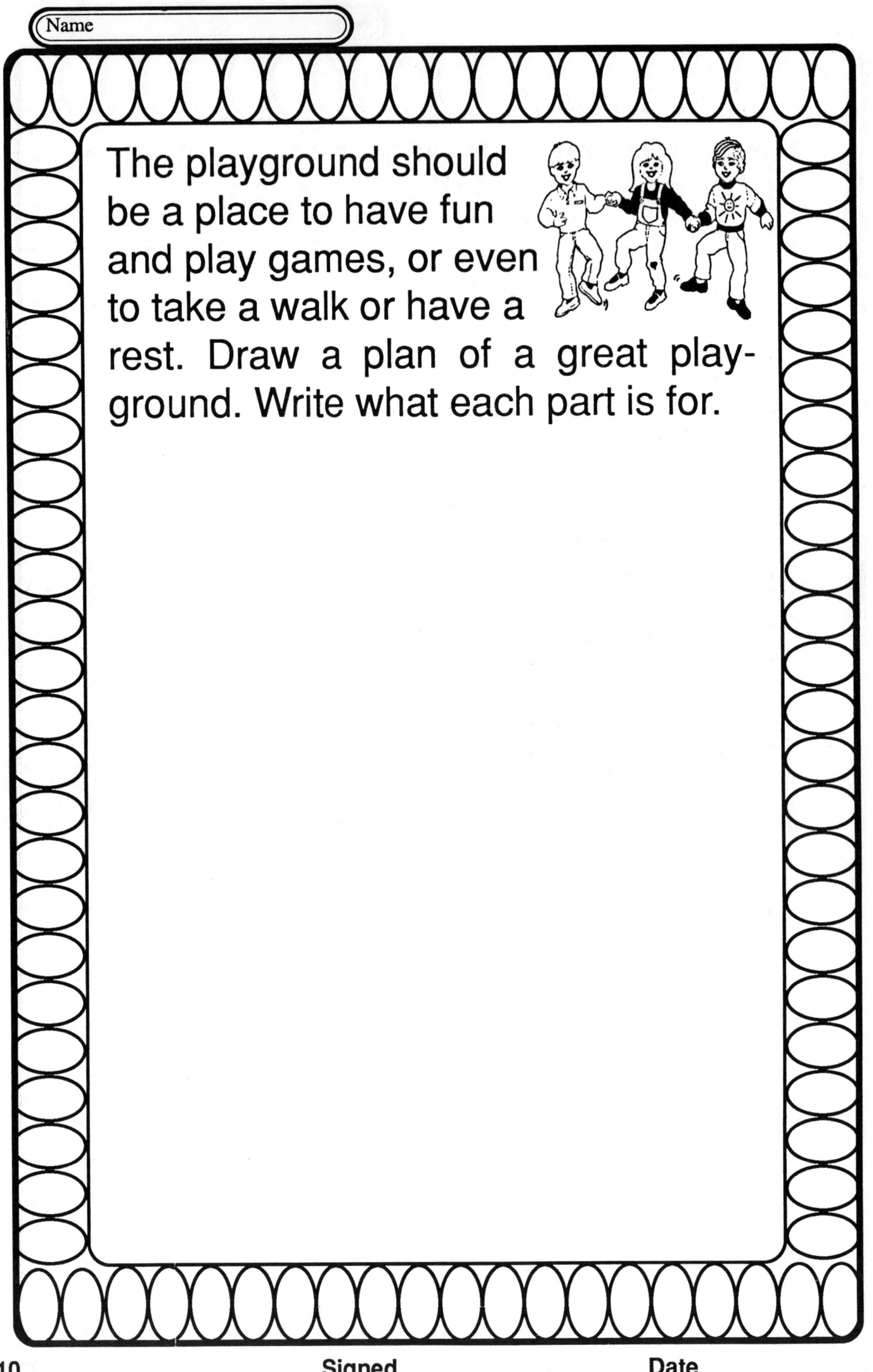

Signed

Date

Think of all the nice things you can call someone. Unjumble the words to see what one boy thought of. Choose from these words:

**good   friendly   nice   gentle   clever
polite   kind   helpful   happy   smart**

rdflinye

_____

levrce

_____

plteio

_____

elngte

_____

ephflul

_____

hpypa

_____

idnk

_____

neci

_____

atmsr

_____

odog

_____

There is no grass on Mars for the Martians to play on. If Martians came to play on the grass at school what would they do? Draw them playing.

Signed   **Date**

Put your litter in the bin. What is in these rubbish bins? Choose from:

straws sweets crispbags
cans   rubbish   paper

e a
r p
p

p _ _ _ _

a g s
r b p s
c   i

_ r _ _ _ b _ _ _ _

r   i
b sh
b u

r _ _ _ _ _ h

e   s
  t s
e   w

_ w _ _ _ _

c   n
  s
  a

_ _ _ _

r   s
s   w
t   a

_ _ _ _ w _

Make badges for these children:

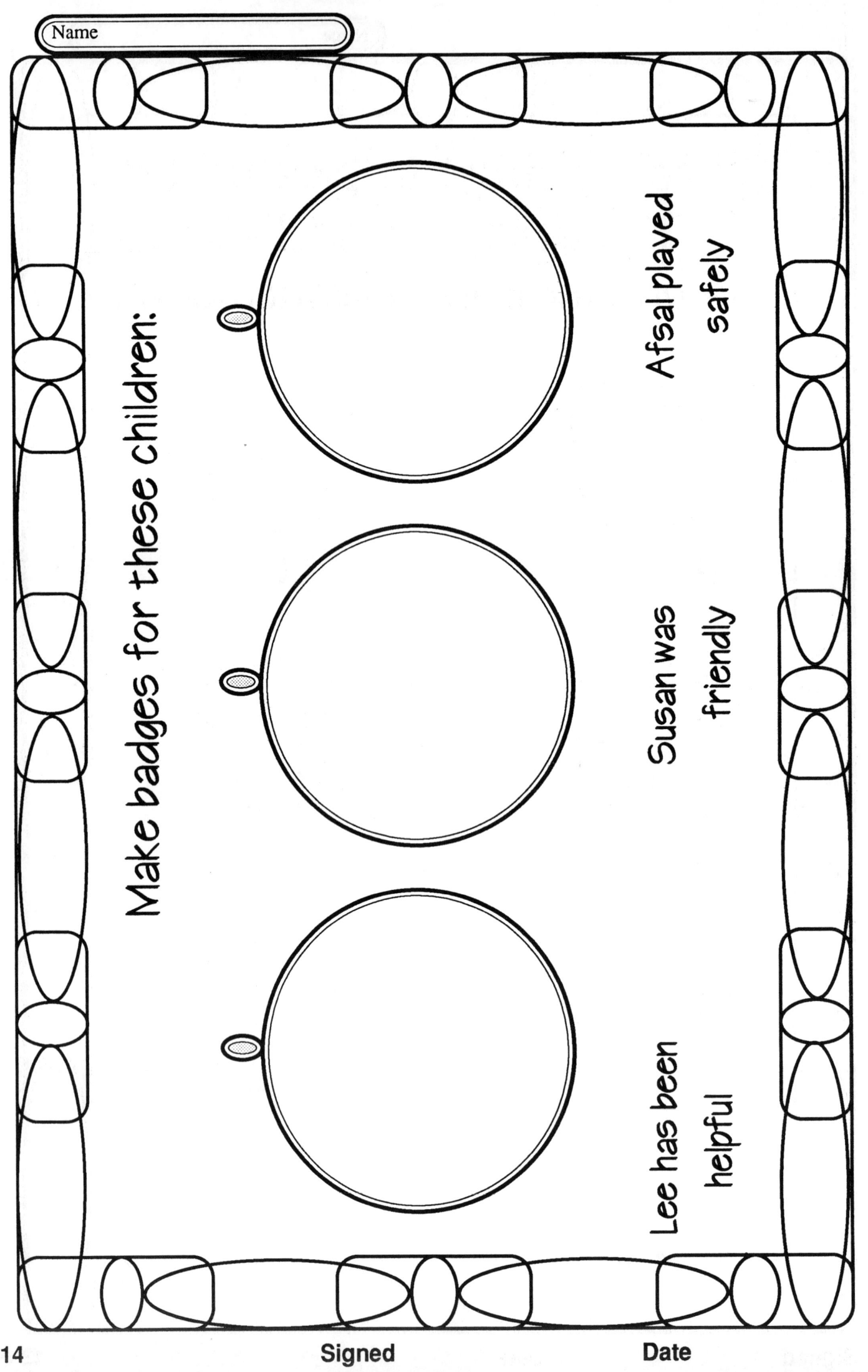

Afsal played safely

Susan was friendly

Lee has been helpful

Signed

Date

Design a robot to pick up the litter in the playground. Label all the working parts on your model.

You would not throw your favourite dinner - it would be a waste.
Draw your best ever meal.

dinner

drink

pudding

Signed

Date

These are good games to play with a ball, but maybe your play space is not big enough. Find the names of the games and write them under each ball. Choose from these games

baseball football rugby
golf rounders cricket tennis

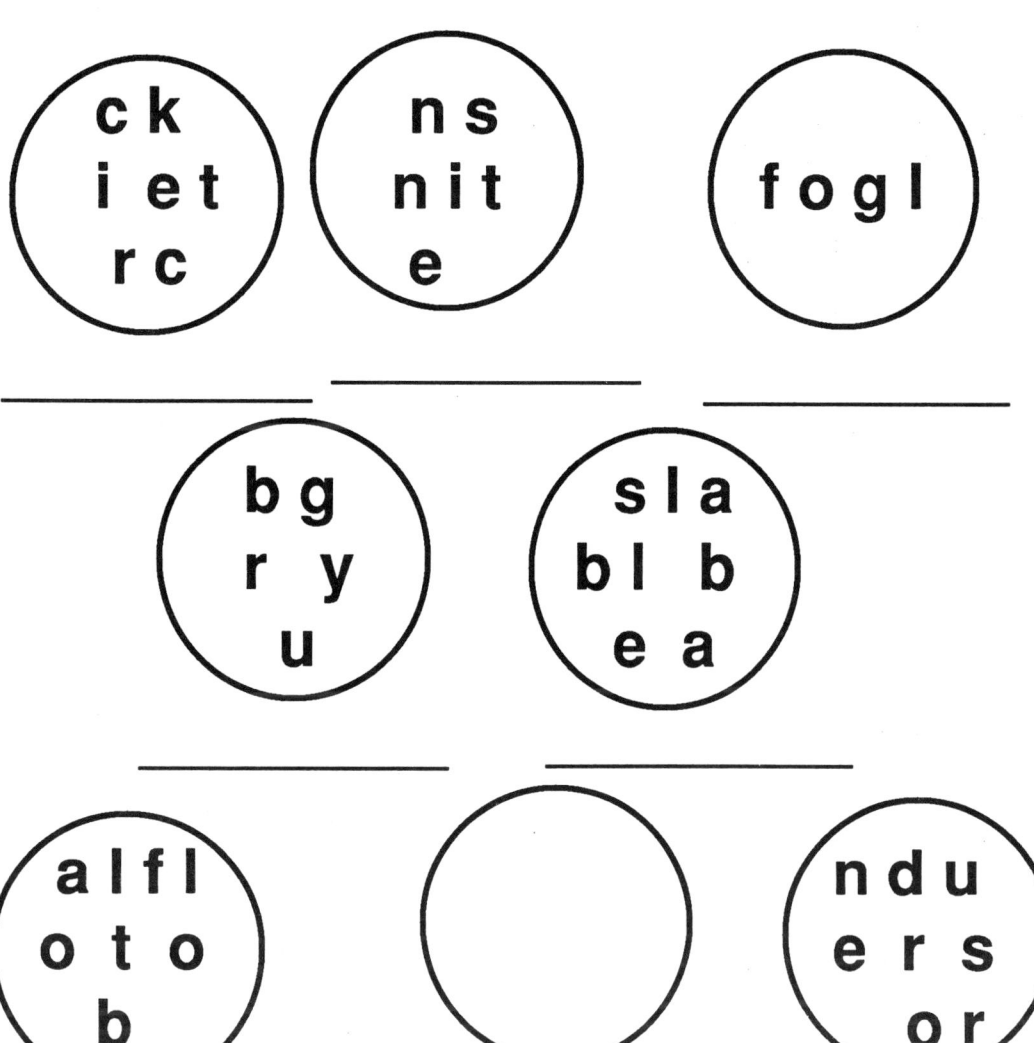

c k
i e t
r c

n s
n i t
e

f o g l

_____ _____ _____

b g
r y
u

s l a
b l b
e a

_____ _____

a l f l
o t o
b

Choose another
game

n d u
e r s
o r

_____ _____

The playground should be a place to have fun and play games. Invent a new playground game. Give it a name and write down how to play it.

Signed

Date

Make a poster to remind all the children about the playground rule: We play safely in the playground without pushing.

Keep your food on your plate. Do not throw it

chips

beans

sausages

peas

Draw the food on each tray.

Put three foods on each plate to make three different meals

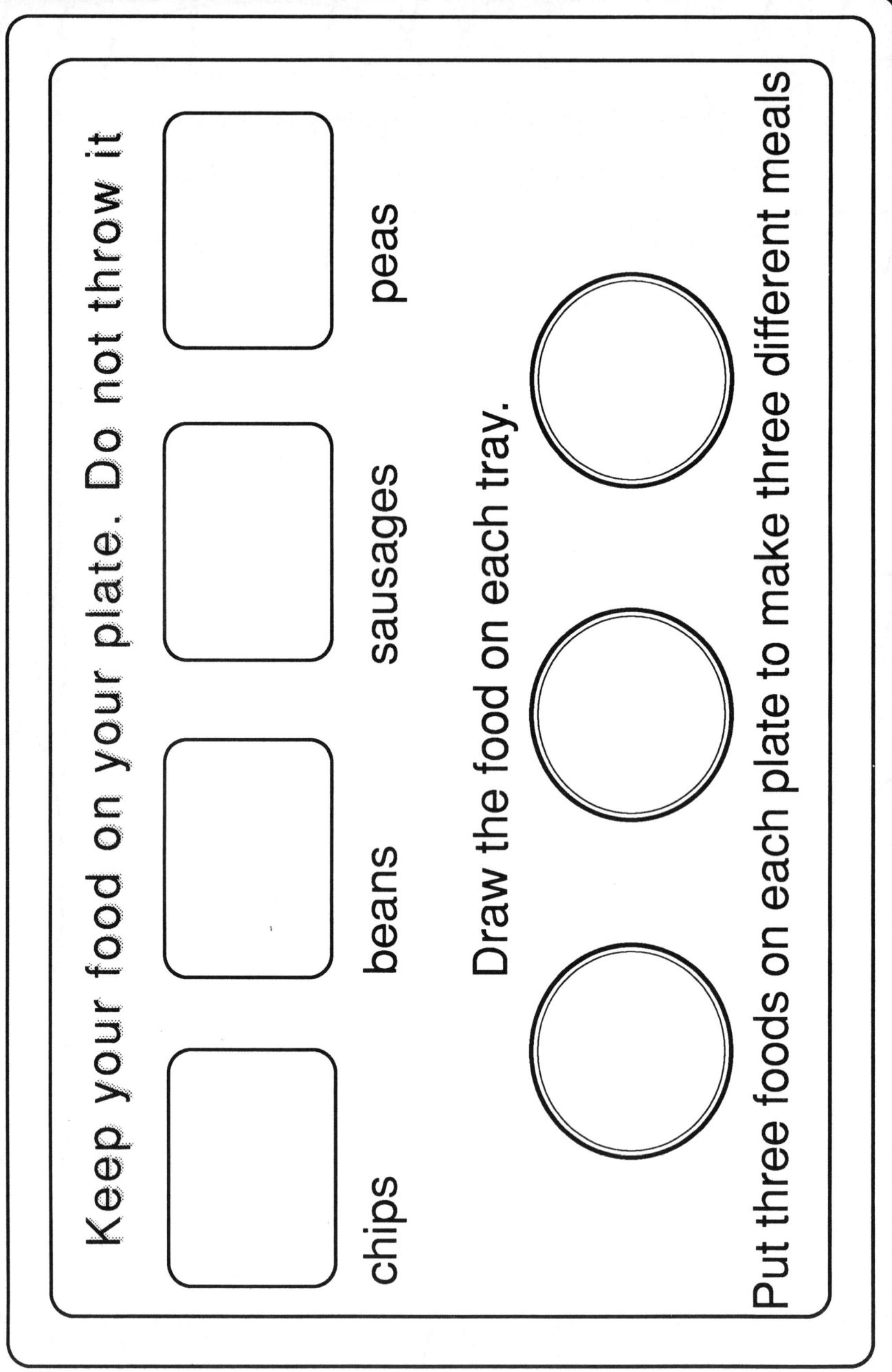

Signed

Date

Make a poster to remind all the
children about the playground rule:
We play safely in the playground
without fighting.

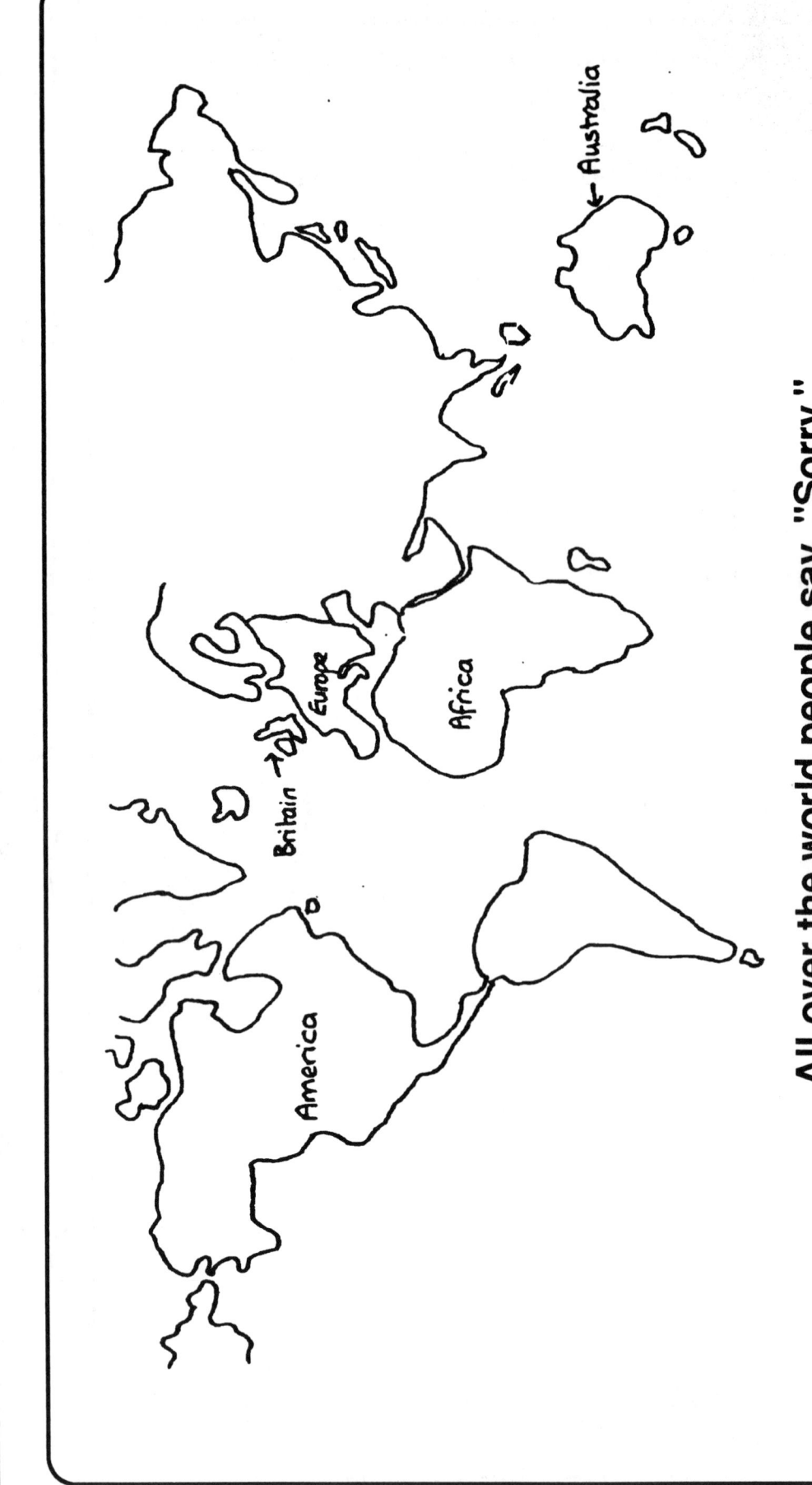

All over the world people say, "Sorry."

Colour in the map.

America - blue: Britain - green: Africa - yellow: Australia - purple: Europe - red.

Try to remember to say "Sorry," when you hurt or upset someone.

Signed **Date**

I should not play in the toilets because:

Draw

I might get wet.

Draw

I might fall and get hurt.

I should not play in the toilets because:

Draw

I might get dirty.

Draw

I might hurt someone.

Signed

Date

If I take somebody else's things from a bag or a drawer, he or she will feel sad or cross.

Draw a cross girl with long dark hair. Make her clothes red and blue

Draw a sad boy.

Make his clothes black and green.

We can use different real names and nicknames.
Nicknames can be friendly or hurtful.
Sort these names and think of some more for each list

fatty Ben dummy   mate   Ann thicky   cow dear sir
star love weedy   John   idiot   pet   dog Sally   creep

real names

friendly names

hurtful names

Signed

Date

There are lots of good games to play with one ball. Invent a new game that you play with a football. Write what you do.

Do not throw stones because:

Draw

You might break a window.

Draw

You might hurt someone.

Signed **Date**

Daily Newspaper

Child hurt climbing at school

Yesterday at a local school a child was badly hurt after climbing on...

Some places are dangerous to climb.

Draw 2 of them

Some places are safe to climb.

Draw 2 of them

Signed

Date

If you play on the grass...

Draw

You might get muddy.

Draw

You might get wet shoes.

If you run in and out of school....

Draw

You might fall over.

Draw

You might knock someone over.

Signed   **Date**

The best thing about playtime is:
Draw 4 things that you like.

Name

Never run in School

Draw 4 places where it is safe to run.

34   **Signed**   **Date**

People who keep to the rules are safe. They also have a good time. Take time to think about the rules for your playground.

Make a picture list of the games you **can** play.

Make a picture list of the games you **cannot** play.

If you play on the grass in your school clothes and shoes they might get dirty. We wear special clothes and shoes to play games on the grass. Draw the right things for these games.

football

cricket

golf

rounders

Signed

Date

What other people think of me:

my friends

my teacher

my parents

the headteacher

dinner ladies

people at home

Name

My friends

Who do you play with at break?
Make the faces into your friends.

[ ] is

a good friend
because

[ ] is

a good friend
because

[ ] is

a good friend
because

Signed

Date

Thinking about you.

You are special. No one in the whole world is the same as you. You are the only one... You are **unique**.

Draw your picture in the frame.

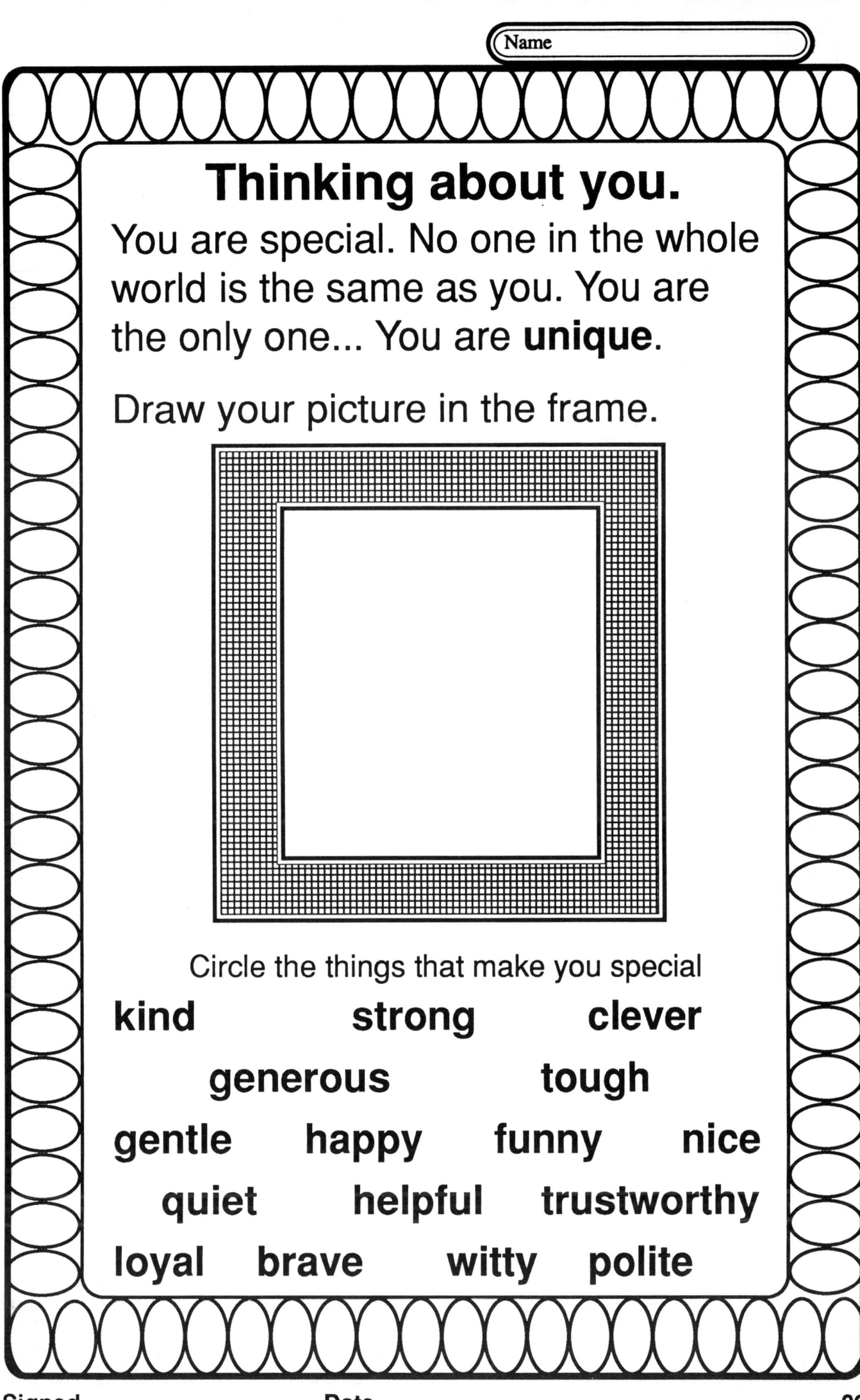

Circle the things that make you special

kind   **strong**   **clever**

generous   **tough**

gentle   **happy**   **funny**   **nice**

quiet   **helpful**   **trustworthy**

loyal   **brave**   **witty**   **polite**

What do you do in the playground?

Put a tick in the right column.

	not much	sometimes	a lot
play with bigger children			
feel sad			
sit quietly			
hate older children			
sit by yourself			
play with friends			
feel frightened			
stay by a dinner lady			
run about			
play alone			
have fun			
feel cross			
play with girls			
play with boys			
stay by a teacher			
play with younger children			

Signed   **Date**

Thinking about Friends

Draw a picture of your best friend.

_____ Name

_____ Age

I like my friend
because

_____

_____

Draw two more friends

Name   Name

Fill in the chart:

	playtime	dinnertime
What do you do?		
Who do you play with?		
Who is on duty?		
What can you do?		
What can't you do?		
Do you like this time?		

Signed **Date**

Draw a map of the play spaces.

Colour the places you like to play.

I play here because....

Mark crosses at the places where you get into trouble.

I get into trouble here because....

School dinner or Packed lunch?

Use the right box and draw your favourite meal Label each food or drink

packed lunch

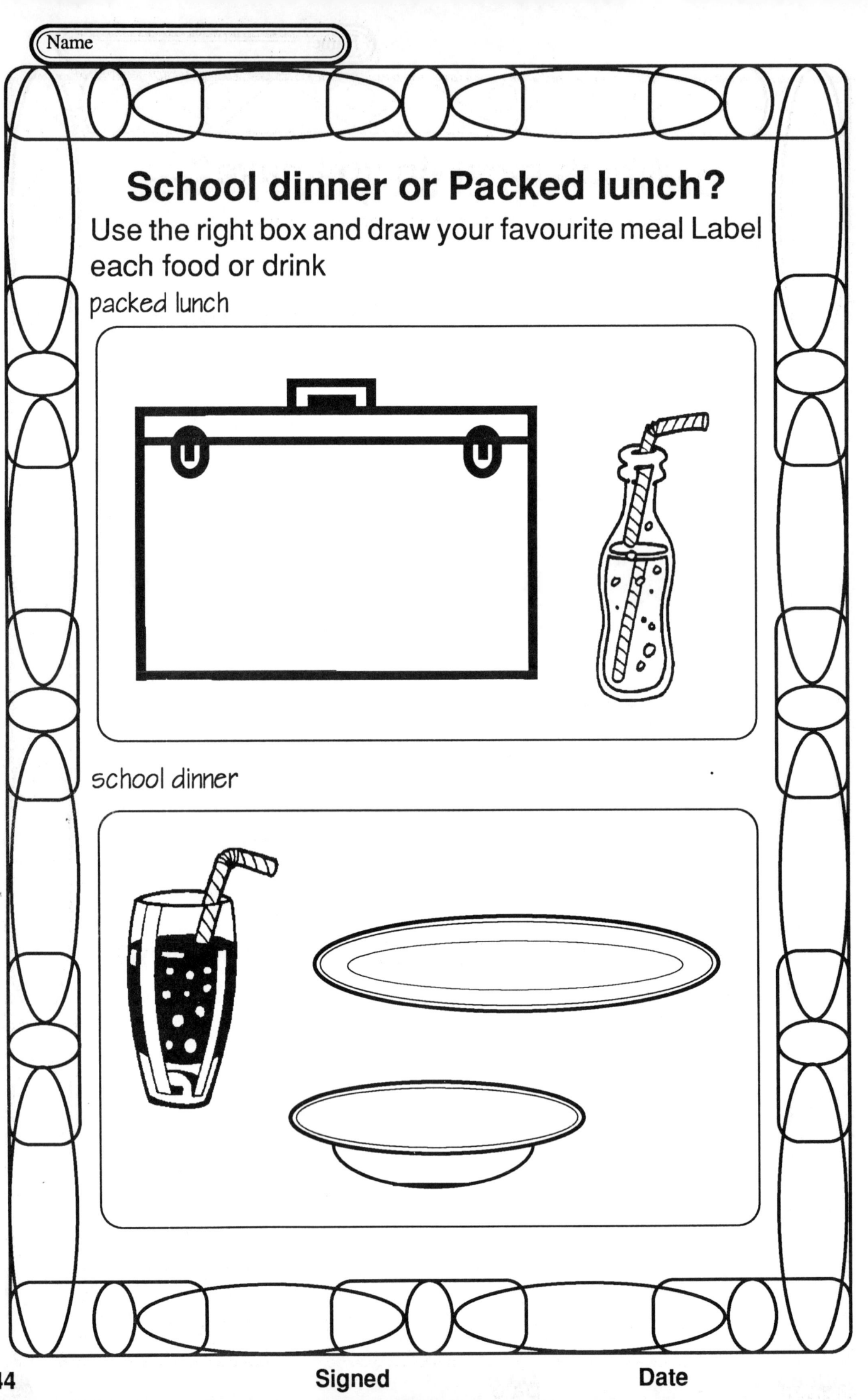

school dinner

Signed   **Date**

Which meal do you have?

Put a circle around the right one.

School Dinner   Packed Lunch

If you could swap for one day what would you like for your meal?

Draw or write what you would eat and drink.

Feelings

Put a blue mark on the line to show how you feel when you get in to trouble in the playground.

Sad _____ **Happy**

Clever _____ **Silly**

Embarrassed _____ **Proud**

Pleased _____ **Cross**

Big _____ **Small**

Confident _____ **Scared**

Now put a red mark on the line to show how you feel when you have behaved well in the playground.

Signed   **Date**

Take time to think!

Why have you been sent in
from the playground?
Use the boxes to show
what happened.

What could you have done to stop it happening?

Information about Friends

Friends are important. They are fun to be with but sometimes we behave worse with our friends. They can be a "bad influence."

List your friends

1
2
3
4
5
6
7

Put them in the right set.

Never in trouble

Often in trouble

Sometimes in trouble

Signed

Date

Sort your friends into these sets:

fun to be with

sometimes nasty to me

Which friends should you play with? Do you need to find some new friends?

Nobody is all bad!

Think of two people you do not like very much. Draw them.

Now think of three good things about the people you have drawn.

1.   1.

2.   2.

3.   3.

Do you know the Rules?
Yes   No

<u>People who understand the rules are:</u>
    * less likely to get into trouble
    * more likely to have good friends
    * more likely to have fun

<u>People who break the rules are:</u>
    * likely to get into trouble
    * a danger to others
    * less likely to enjoy themselves
    * less likely to have friends

Write down the rules you know for the playground. Put a tick by the rules you keep.

    1.

    2.

    3.

    4.

    5.

In trouble again!

Think of three reasons why you have been in trouble. Draw a cartoon for each time.

Why do you getting into trouble?

What can you do to stop getting into trouble?

Signed

Date

Choose 4 things you like doing in the playground. Put a ring round them.

singing   hiding   balancing

running   ballgames

chasing   sitting   climbing

football   watching

jumping   talking   marbles

swinging   pretend games

shouting   skipping   resting

Do these things get you into trouble?

yes   no   sometimes

Write why?

Draw the headteacher.

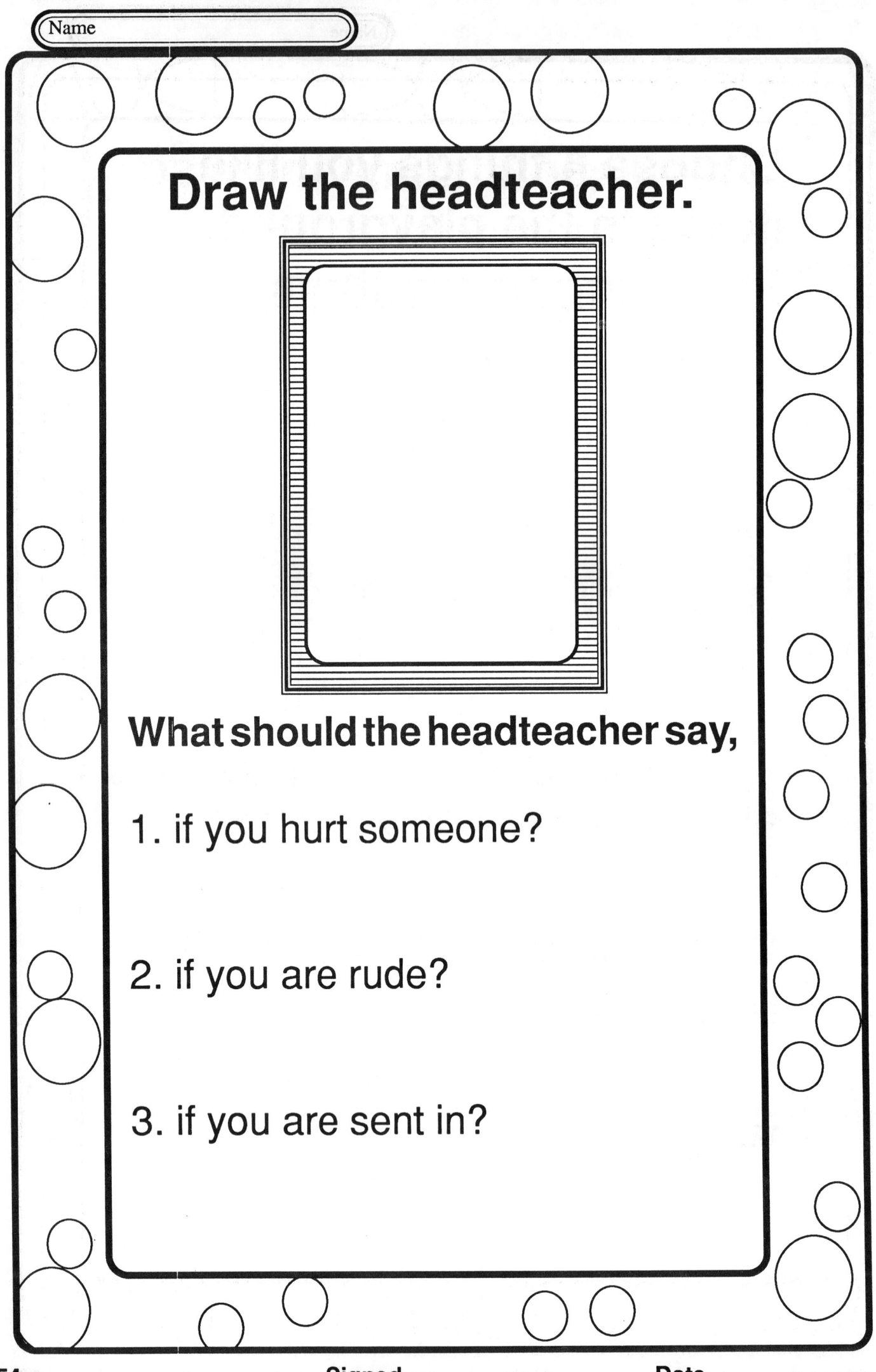

What should the headteacher say,

1. if you hurt someone?

2. if you are rude?

3. if you are sent in?

Signed   **Date**

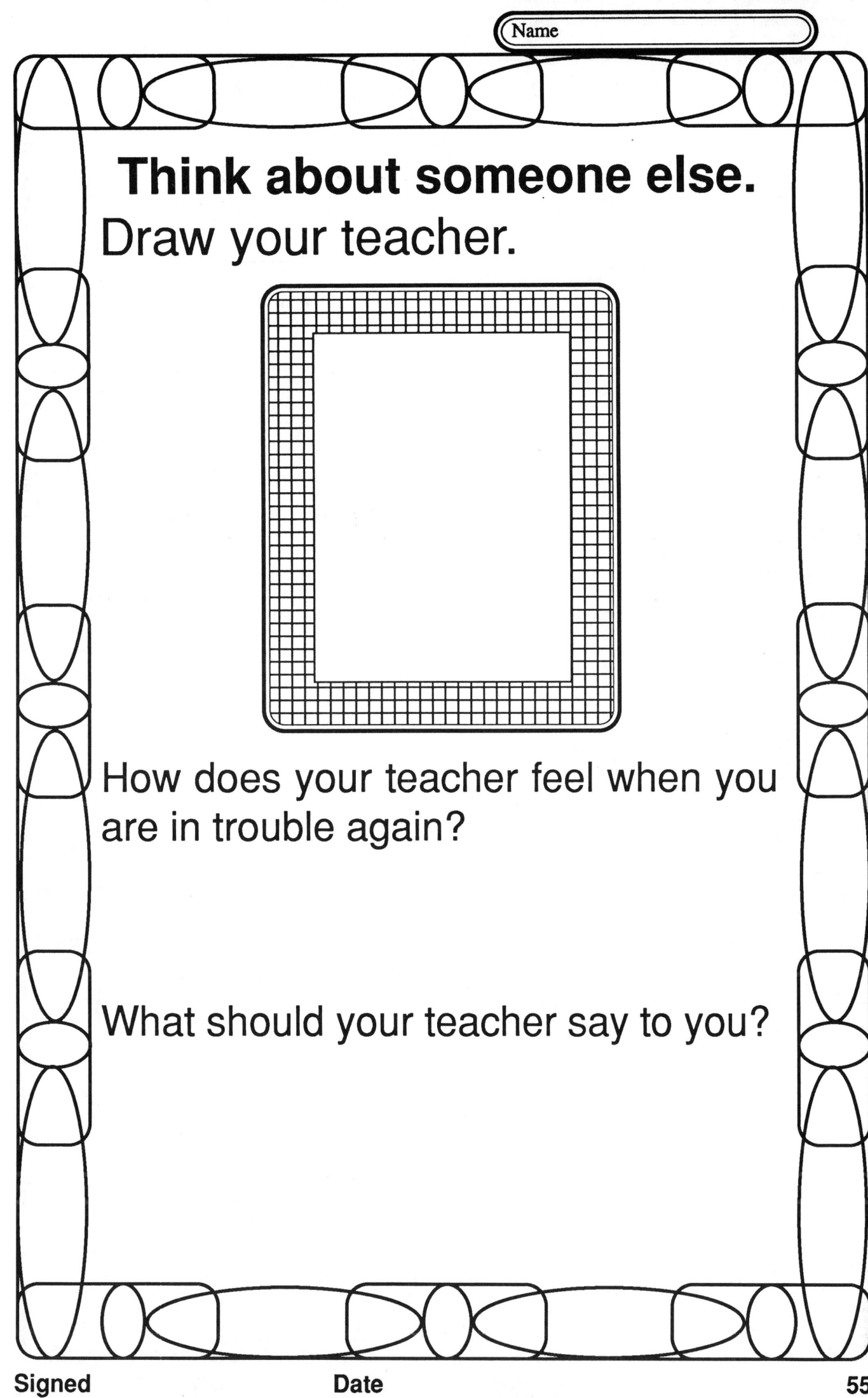

Think about someone else.

Draw your teacher.

How does your teacher feel when you are in trouble again?

What should your teacher say to you?

Think!

What would you do if...

Someone knocked you over on purpose?

Someone knocked you over by accident?

Someone frightens you?

Someone says something rude about your family?

Are you ideas good or will they get you into trouble? Put a tick by all the good ideas and a cross by the bad ones.

Signed **Date**

Think!
What would you do if...

You saw two boys fighting?

You saw a big girl pushing a little girl?

You saw a little child crying?

You saw someone alone with nobody to play with?

Helping others.

These children need help.
How could you help them?
Draw the people and write what you would say.

I've fallen down
My leg is cut.

Nobody will
play with me

Signed **Date**

Helping others.

These children need help.
How could you help them?
Draw the people and write what you would say.

Thinking about somebody else.

Somebody has fallen over. Use the cartoon strip to show what you should do to help.

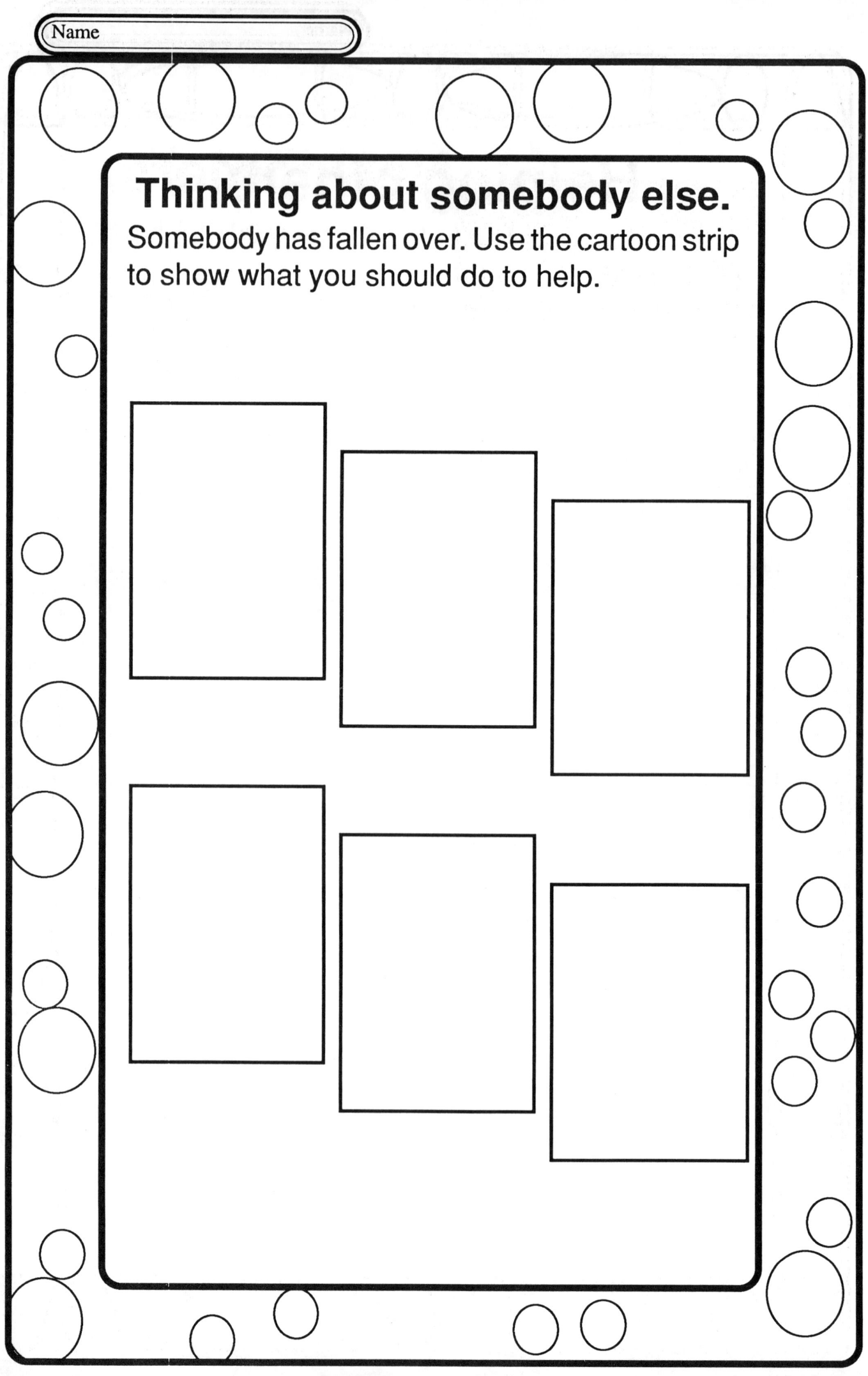

Signed **Date**

Newcomers.

A new child has come to your school who **hates** playtimes. What could you do to help?

Draw your ideas.

Helping Ashley

Ashley is always in trouble.
Nobody will play with Ashley
Ashley is fed up.
Ashley wants friends to play with.
Ashley needs help.

What do you suggest?

Signed
Date

Making new friends

Here are some ideas for making new friends.
Draw the pictures to show what you would do.

I could help somebody who might be my friend

I could share my crisps or my snack at breaktime.

I could ask him or her to join in my game.

Telling Jokes.

Getting into trouble is no fun at all. It is better to do things that people like.

Telling jokes is a good way to make people laugh and feel friendly.

Draw the cartoons for these jokes.

Why did the hedgehog have dandruff?
Because he left his head and shoulders on the motorway.

Why did the golfer wear two pairs of trousers?
Because he had a hole in one.

Put two more jokes in these boxes and tell them at breaktime.

Signed

Date

Limericks

People who can entertain others are usually popular. Limericks or loopy rhymes are a good way to make your friends laugh.

Learn this limerick.

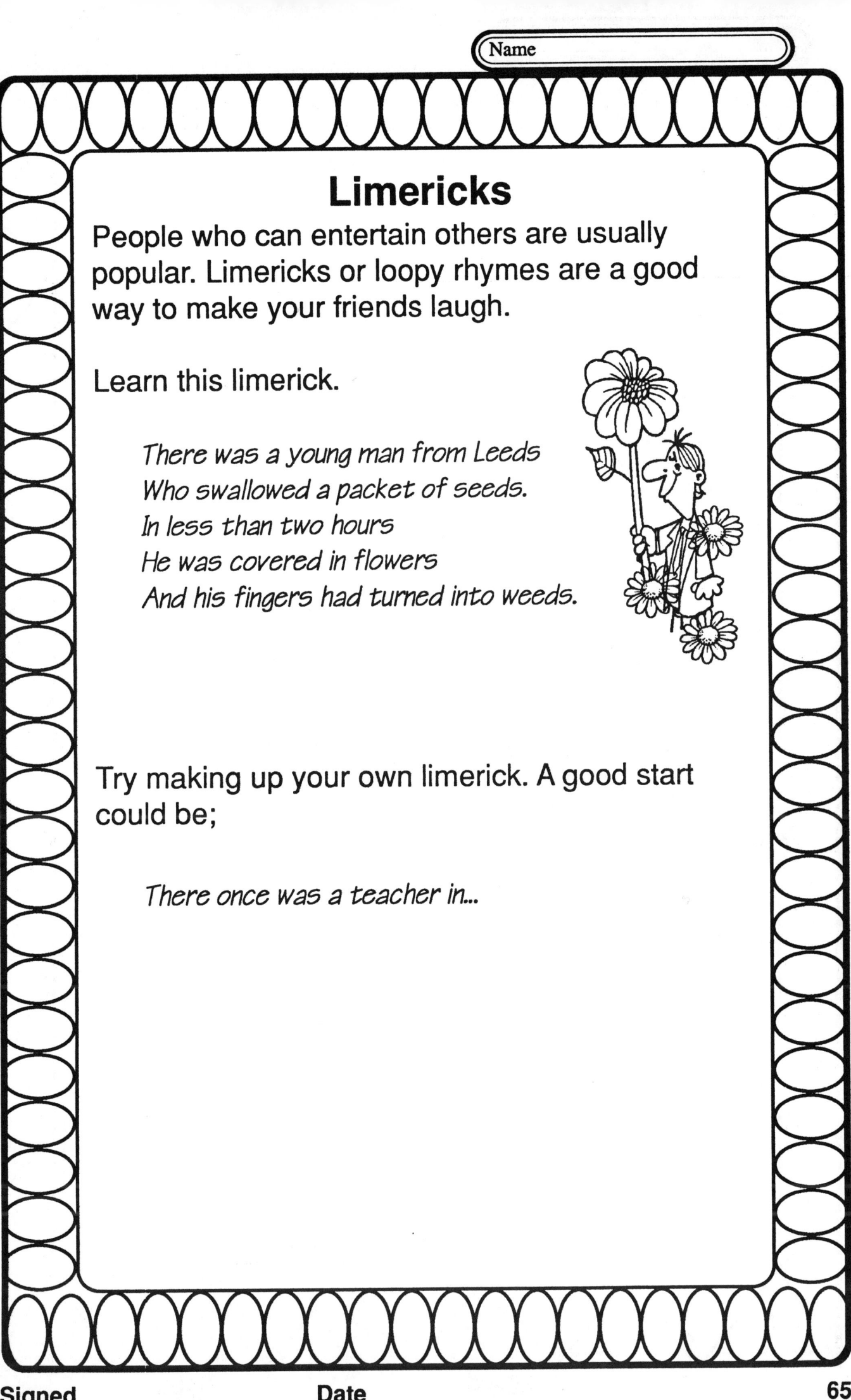

There was a young man from Leeds
Who swallowed a packet of seeds.
In less than two hours
He was covered in flowers
And his fingers had turned into weeds.

Try making up your own limerick. A good start could be;

There once was a teacher in...

Name

Signed

Date

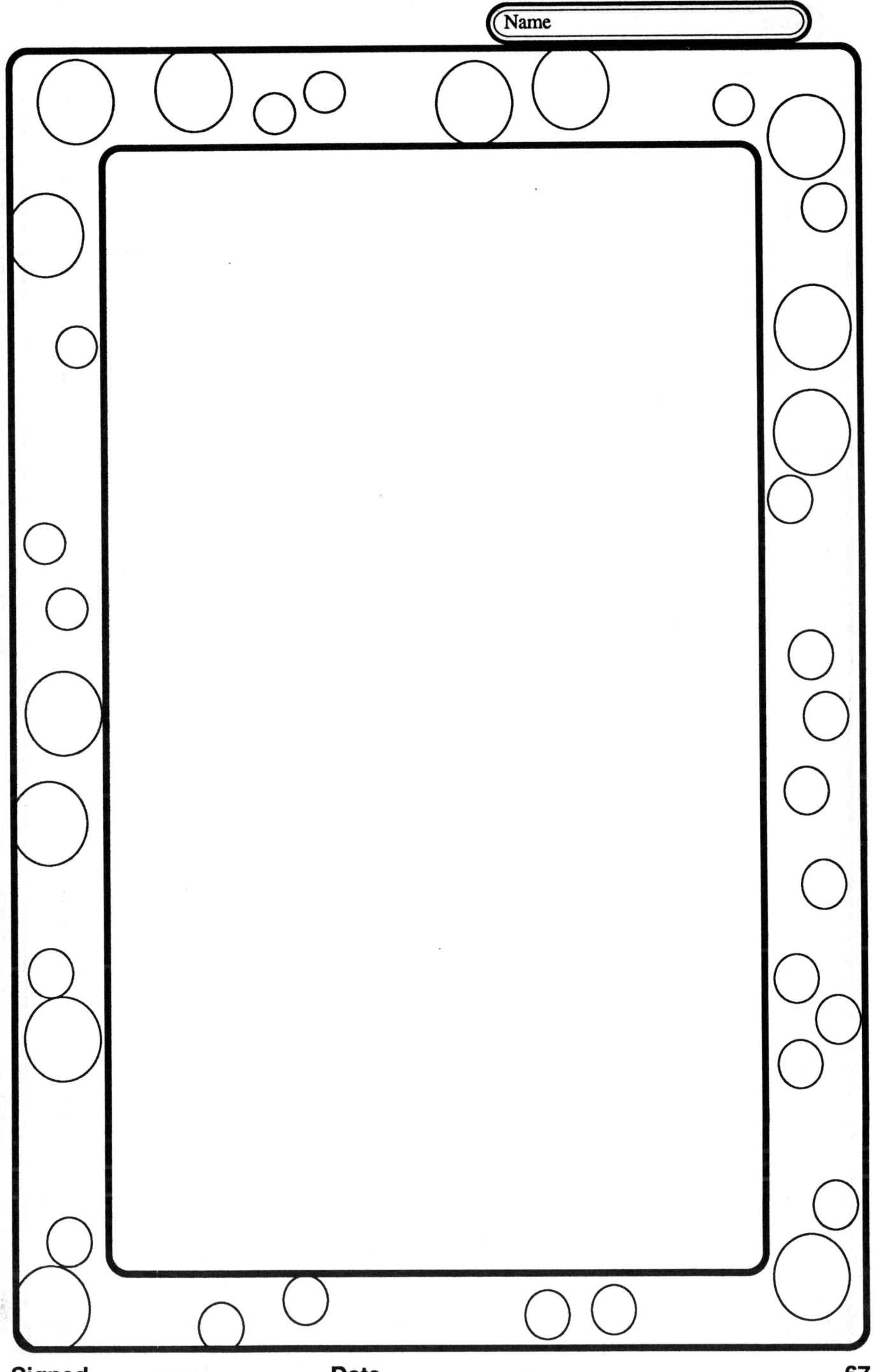

Name

Signed   Date   67

Name

Signed

Date

Name

Signed   **Date**   69

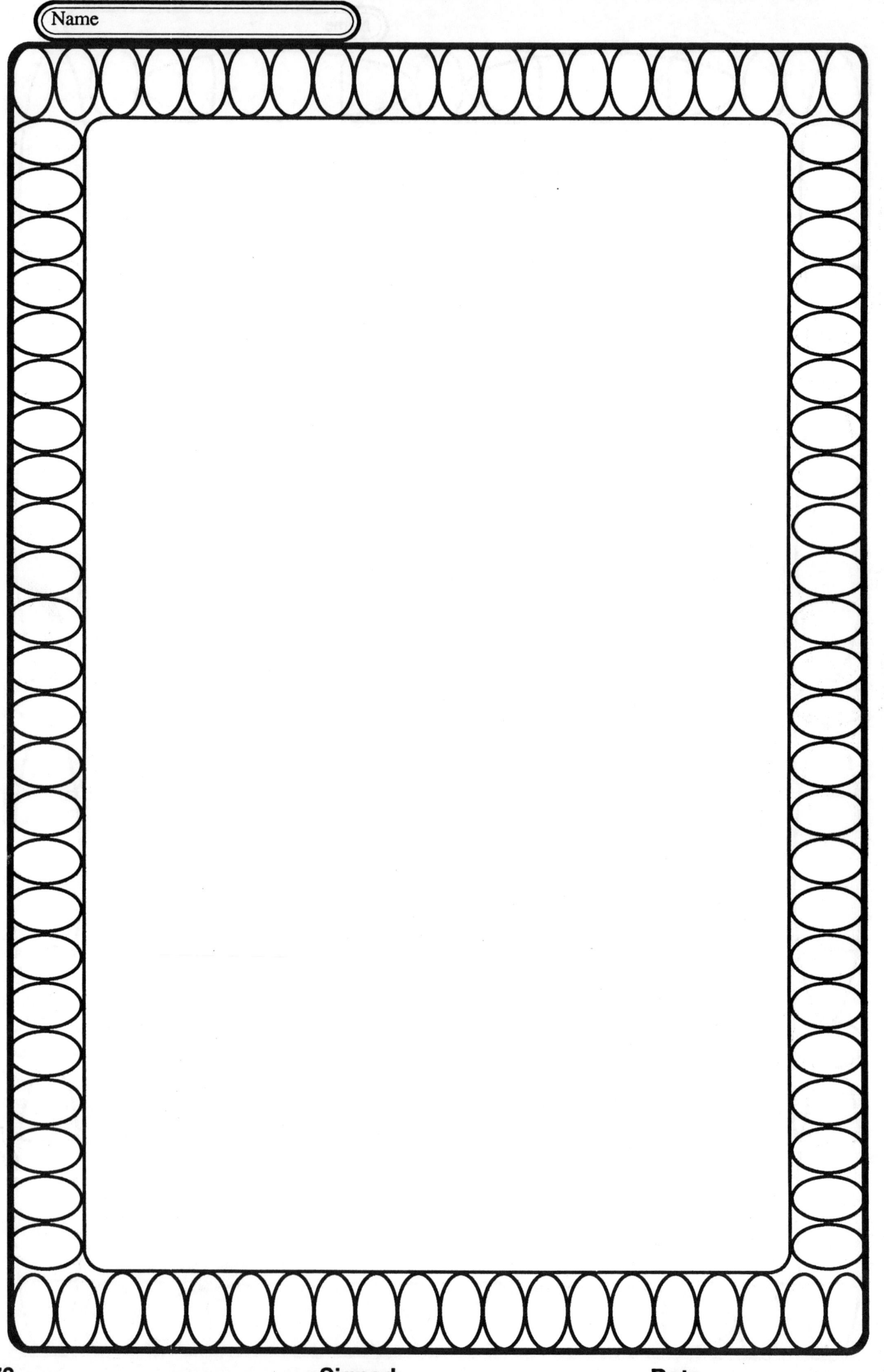

Name

Signed

Date